# Amazing Bu[g, Frog and Bird Tales]

# *Amazing But True* Cat Tales

Bruce Nash and Allan Zullo

Compiled by Muriel MacFarlane

Andrews and McMeel * *A Universal Press Syndicate Company* * Kansas City

Design by Rick Cusick
Illustrations by Paul Coker, Jr.

Library of Congress Cataloging–in–Publication Data

Nash, Bruce M.
    Amazing but true cat tales / Bruce Nash and Allan Zullo ; compiled
by Muriel MacFarlane.
        p.    cm.
    ISBN 0-8362-8034-2 : $6.95
    1. Cats—Anecdotes.  2. Cats—Miscellanea.  I. Zullo, Allan.
II. MacFarlane, Muriel.  III. Title.
SF445.5.N37
636.8—dc20                                        93-11381
                                                    CIP

Attention: Schools and Businesses
Andrews and McMeel books are available at quantity discounts with bulk purchase for educational, business, or sales promotional use. For information, please write to: Special Sales Department, Andrews and McMeel, 4900 Main Street, Kansas City, Missouri 64112.

# Dedication

To Mary Williams, a purr-fectly wonderful
sister-in-law.

> —*Bruce Nash*

To Steve and Barb Arnold, who for years
gave such heartfelt T.L.C. to L.C.L.

> —*Allan Zullo*

To J.D., D.D., and Edward Eugene. Thinking
of you helps me overcome the hairballs of life.

> —*Muriel MacFarlane*

# Acknowledgments

There are several people without whom the material for this book never could have been assembled.

Special thanks go to Jennifer and Joe Cardozo, Dottie Duffy, Sandi Juni, Catharine Rambeau, Shirley Spear, Ellie Silverman, and Joe Whiteman.

# Contents

*Cats make the most intriguing pets . . .*

# Cats Incredible!

*They are alternately charming and cunning, affectionate and aloof, obedient and stubborn. They are loyal, playful, and sweet—but only when they want to be. They've been domesticated for some 3,000 years . . . and we still haven't figured them out!*

*But there's one thing about cats that we all know: They are incredible creatures.*

*This book is a celebration of fantastic felines whose antics and adventures will astound and amuse you. Like the devoted Siamese who trudged 1,400 miles over four years to be reunited with his family . . . the lucky cat who plunged out of a twenty-story apartment building and walked off with only minor injuries . . . the courageous feline who saved a helpless poodle from the deadly jaws of a pit bull . . . the resourceful stray who helped build the Grand Coulee Dam.*

*In our research, we found remarkable stories of cats who've been showered with tons of love. For instance, two felines inherited a $750,000 luxury condo in New York . . . a pampered pet was thrown an extravagant $10,000 birthday party . . . and twenty adopted felines had a $100,000 cat house built especially for them.*

*We also found wacky accounts of cats who wound up in big trouble. For example, a pussy got collared by the cops after repeatedly dialing 911 . . . a roaming cat was put under house arrest by a judge . . . and one hundred felines broke up the marriage of their owner.*

*Whether strays, purebreds, or mongrels, these four-legged animals are always up to something—as characters in the most amazing but true cat tales!*

# Vagabond Cats
### ...Who Found Their Way Home

**A Purrfect Ending**

In one of the most astonishing cases of feline devotion, a Siamese cat named Sam took four years to travel more than 1,400 miles to be reunited with his owners.

Linda Thompson and her sons brought their cat with them when they moved from Beaver Dam, Wisconsin, to Tucson, Arizona, in 1986. A year later, the family was in such financial distress that they returned to Beaver Dam to live. But because they couldn't afford to keep Sam, they left the three-year-old cat behind at the Tucson Humane Society in the hope that he would be adopted.

The Thompsons thought that was the last they'd ever see of Sam. They were wrong.

Sam loved his owners so much that he was determined to find them. After somehow managing to escape, he set out on an incredible trek to return to his family.

Amazingly, in 1991—four years and 1,429 miles later—Sam showed up at the back doorstep of the Beaver Dam house where the Thompsons used to live! A few days later, the new home owners told Linda Thompson about her cat.

"I thought nothing of it, but my son Joe went over there and nearly flipped," recalled Linda. "It was Sam all right. Joe could tell by his markings. When I saw Sam, he jumped right into my arms. He looked a little skinny, but otherwise he was fine. We've been in shock ever since. We have no idea how he did it. But one thing is for sure. We're never going anywhere without Sam again."

## A Tale of Two Kitties

A house cat that wanted no part of the family's vacation retreat ran away and trudged 773 miles in seven months just to get back home! And in another remarkable incident, a pet feline took twenty-two months to return to his owner's holiday home.

In 1986, Jeanene Brock and her husband took their black-and-white cat, Tom, with them when they left their home in Lincoln Park, Michigan, a suburb of Detroit, to spend the winter in Harrison, Arkansas.

When they arrived at their vacation home, Jeanene recalled, "Tom was so anxious to stretch his legs that I felt sorry for him and let him out. I've had Tom since he was only days old. I raised him from a bottle, so I never dreamed that he would take off. But he did.

"I couldn't sleep at night because I kept thinking about him. I spent many nights tossing and turning, praying for my poor Tom's return."

Her prayers were eventually answered.

Remarkably, seven months after he vanished, the footloose feline showed up—scratching at the window of Jeanene's Lincoln Park neighbor! "When I saw the cat, I knew immediately that it was Tom because he had a distinctive black-and-white marking," said the neighbor, Mrs. Lois Wickman.

She called Jeanene's twenty-two-year-old son, Glen Daniels, with the news, and he rushed right over. "To my amazement, there was Tom," he recalled. "He was ecstatic to be home because he licked my face, rubbed against me, and purred to beat the band."

Daniels took the cat to veterinarian Dr. Rene Deptula, who treated the pet for a bite wound and a few sores. "Tom had lost a few pounds and was a little ragged, but otherwise was in good condition," said the vet. "How did he find his way back without getting lost? Instinct."

Beamed Jeanene: "Tom is a miracle cat."

Although Tom may not have wanted to stay in a vacation home, a house cat in France walked over 250 miles in twenty-two months just so he could enjoy the family's holiday retreat.

In the spring of 1990, Patrice and Michele Craye of Paris made their annual visit to their vacation home in LeTourneur, France. But it was the first time in several years that they hadn't taken their pet, Mimine, with them on their holiday. Instead, they left him behind with one of their sons.

**13**

But when the couple returned home, they discovered that Mimine unexplainably had run away. The Crayes searched for a month, but could not find their beloved cat.

In time, the heartbroken family grew to accept life without their pet and bought another tabby to fill the void. But they were still so attached to their long-gone cat that they named their new feline after him—Mimine II.

Nearly two years later, during another holiday, the Crayes returned to their vacation home in LeTourneur. This time, they brought along Mimine II. A day later, the Crayes received the shock of their lives.

There, on the front doorstep of their house, was a dirty, frail tabby that looked suspiciously like the first Mimine! When their son, Bertrand, called his name, Mimine leaped into his arms.

The courageous cat had traveled 250 miles through fields, over roads, into woods, and even across the Seine River to reach the Crayes's vacation home. He was skin and bones and walked with a limp, but otherwise he was fine.

*Abraham Lincoln rescued three young cats*
*that he found half-frozen in General Grant's*
*camp during the Civil War.*

## The Cat Who Swallowed the Canaries

Murka the house cat was banished from her home after she ate two canaries. But time—and a 400-mile journey—earned forgiveness from her master.

Murka shared a quiet, contented life in a small Moscow apartment with her owner, Vladimir Dontsov. But then in 1988, Dontsov—paying little heed to feline instincts—brought home two canaries to live with him.

The birds were just too much of a temptation for Murka. One day, while Dontsov was at work, she knocked over the bird cage. When it crashed to the floor, the cage door sprang open and the canaries flew for their lives inside the apartment. But they didn't have a chance. Murka, doing what her ancestors had done for thousands of years, chased after the birds. She captured and ate the first canary. Then she pounced on the second one and devoured it.

Stuffed and satisfied, she took a nap, only to be roused by angry shouts from her master when he returned home to discover the carnage. Dontsov was so upset that he banished Murka from his home. But rather than kick her out in the street, he sent the cat to live with his relatives in Voronezh, 400 miles south of Moscow.

But two days after she arrived at her new home, Murka disappeared. When Dontsov heard the news, he felt guilty about dumping her. Then he wondered what fate had befallen his former house cat.

A year later, he found out. As Dontsov stepped into the lobby of his apartment building, he couldn't believe his eyes. There in the corner was Murka—dirty, hungry, pregnant, and missing part of her tail. He scooped her up in his arms and hugged her. "I'll never let you go again," he shouted.

According to the Russian newspaper *Komsomolskaya Pravda*, Murka has become a celebrity in her apartment building, having survived a long, perilous journey—and a harsh Russian winter. "She is back home now," said the newspaper. "She is admired and respected for her tenacity, and the canary-eating incident has been forgiven."

### VIPs (Very Important Pets)

Twice in 1991, missing cats returned home in style—by flying first-class on a commercial jet.

A plump Himalayan cat, whose full name is Irving Robinowitz, escaped from his carrying case while it was being placed in the cargo hold of a Continental Airlines jet at Newark International Airport. The flight was delayed for more than an hour while airport workers frantically searched for the fleeing feline.

To avoid further delaying the other frustrated passengers, the cat's heartsick owners, Helen and Ralph Roselli, asked Continental to take off without their pet. But two hours into the flight, the pilot made an announcement: "Mr. and Mrs. Roselli, they found Irving and we'll fly him back tomorrow—first class."

To celebrate, the flight attendants served free booze to the passengers, who had cheered and applauded the pilot's good news.

True to their word, Continental officials—who found Irving in the employee's break room—flew the cat home to West Palm Beach, Florida, the next day and into the waiting arms of his owners.

Months earlier, a cat named Bobby had a much more harrowing experience before he was given the VIP treatment.

Bobby wandered away from his home to nearby Houston Intercontinental Airport, where he climbed into an unheated, unpressurized wheel compartment of a Pan Am jet. Incredibly, he survived the extremely thin air and below-zero outside temperatures on the 1,700-mile trip to New York City.

After the plane landed, mechanic Gary Hickman heard loud meowing coming from the landing gear and discovered the greasy, scared, but unharmed Bobby. "I thought, 'Holy cow! How could this little guy still be alive?'" recalled Hickman, who gave the shaking cat oxygen and milk.

Bobby was turned over to a feline-loving pilot, Paul Scholz, who flew the cat home on a bundle of blankets in his plane's cockpit and fed him a dinner of poached salmon. "It's a miracle Bobby survived the flight and didn't fall out when the landing gear was lowered," said Scholz.

Back in Houston, the pilot found Bobby's owner, Elaine Nolan, through the cat's rabies tag. "I think it's all so crazy," she said. "But I'm just so glad Bobby's home."

*The first visitor that Louis XV allowed in his bedroom every morning was his white cat.*

# Never-Say-Die Cats

## ...Who Led Nine Lives

### Concrete Evidence

Joey, a green-eyed tabby, accidentally was buried alive under eight inches of concrete. Yet miraculously the feisty feline survived! Refusing to give up, Joey kept clawing away at the cement until finally, after eleven exhausting days, he broke through to freedom.

In 1992, Joey, a house cat owned by six-year-old Kimberly Webb of Madison, Wisconsin, had wandered out of the family's first-floor apartment, where workers were repairing a patio. That was the last anyone had seen of the cat.

When he failed to show up for dinner, Kimberly was crushed. "I cried a lot because I was so sad," she recalled. "I wanted to see my kitty again."

For days, Kimberly scoured the neighborhood, stopping everyone she saw and asking if they had seen her tabby. The answer was always the same: No. She and her mother, Ira Webb, posted lost pet signs throughout the area, but there was no sign of Joey.

Then on Easter Sunday—eleven days after he disappeared and just when Kimberly was ready to give up—a bedraggled Joey appeared at the Webbs' patio door. "We couldn't believe it," recalled Kimberly's mother.

Kimberly was overjoyed. "My mom said I was so surprised that my eyes got as big as tomatoes." But Kimberly wasn't half as happy to see Joey as the cat was to see his food bowl. "He went straight to the kitchen and ate like crazy."

Added her mother: "We had to open a can of tuna fish, because after all this time I hadn't bought any more cat food."

Once the Webbs got over the happy shock of Joey's return, they noticed the cat's claws were worn down to the nubs and his paws were full of cement. "He had so much mud and cement on his paws it looked like he was wearing boxing gloves," said Mrs. Webb. Then they examined the recently laid cement and noticed a hole near one corner that wasn't there the day before. Only then did they figure out what had happened.

Their five-year-old cat had wound up in trouble by engaging in his favorite pastime—chasing mice into holes around the Webbs' patio. When maintenance workers began filling in washed-away dirt around the patio slab, Joey became startled. He hid in what he thought was a safe place—a hole in the ground by the edge of the patio. The workers then unwittingly buried the cat when they poured an eight-inch slab of patio concrete over the hole.

For the next eleven days, Joey desperately kept scratching his way toward freedom.

Marveled Thomas Scott, maintenance supervisor at the Webbs' apartment complex, "You should have seen Joey—he didn't have any claws left. They were down to nothing from scratching his way out. He's lucky. I think he must've used up a lot of his nine lives on that little adventure."

## Cat on a Hot-Rod Roof

Housewife Twyla Thompson sped down a highway, fleeing from a strange man who was chasing her.

The fifty-year-old Pebble Beach, California, woman was driving alone in her station wagon one day in 1991 when she saw the man in a dark automobile gesturing frantically, flashing his lights, and signaling her to pull over.

"It's a maniac or a serial killer," Twyla feared as she floored her car and roared off. But the man sped after her in hot pursuit.

Finally, she pulled into a housing development where a security guard was stationed. Twyla hoped this would scare off the nut. But before she had a chance to utter a word, the guard shouted at her, "Lady, you've got a cat on the top of your car!"

Getting out to look, Twyla was stunned to find her cat Panda spread-eagled on the car's roof, hanging onto the luggage rack for dear life. Poor Panda had to be pried loose because his claws were still wrapped around the rack in a determined death-defying grip.

After hugging her still-shaken pet and apologizing to the stranger who was chasing her, Twyla explained that Panda often sunbathed on the roof of the car when it was parked in the driveway. He liked to soak up the sun's rays and the heat that reflected off the car's roof. When she got into the car that day and drove off, Twyla failed to notice the cat was napping on the luggage rack.

Panda no longer goes near the car. When it looks like Twyla is going for a ride, Panda puts his rear in gear and hightails it.

***

Buttons the cat experienced a wild ride too—300 miles under the hood of a car on its engine!

In 1983, the eight-year-old black cat, belonging to Maureen Smith of Great Yarmouth, England, somehow managed to climb onto the engine of a car owned by neighbor Fraser Robertson. The feline was napping under the hood when Robertson drove off for a business trip to Aberdeen, Scotland.

Buttons wasn't discovered until six hours later, when Robertson stopped at a service station in Newcastle and lifted the hood to check on the oil. To his stunned surprise, Robertson found the cat, covered with grime, crouching behind the battery. "How she survived six hours of nonstop driving I will never know," he told reporters later. "The engine was incredibly hot, and what with the petrol fumes, oil smoke, and the noise, it must have been a terrifying experience for her."

Robertson fed the feline at a nearby restaurant and then continued on his trip, this time with Buttons curled up in the backseat of his car. When he reached Aberdeen, Robertson phoned Mrs. Smith with the news about her cat.

Soon, Buttons and her mistress were happily reunited.

## Thundercat

In 1965, a tomcat named Pussycat owned by Anne Walker suddenly leaped through an open window from his eleventh-floor home in London, England, when he was startled by a thunderclap—and fell 120 feet. Fortunately, all he suffered was a fractured right leg, and he made a full recovery. Because of his remarkable free-fall, Pussycat was made a lifetime member of the British Parachute Association.

*In the Ozarks years ago, it was not uncommon for young women pondering a marriage proposal to "leave it to the cat." The girl would take three hairs from a cat's tail, wrap them in paper, and put them under her doorstep. The next morning, she would unfold the paper carefully, trying not to disturb the hairs. If they were arranged similar to a "Y", she should say yes. If they more closely resembled an "N", she should decline the proposal.*

**Feline Fallout**

For some bizarre reason in 1973, cats seemed to experience a falling-out—literally.

During that one year, three cats survived the greatest accidental plunges off apartment balconies in North America.

On April 21, in Toronto, Ontario, Canada, a female cat named Quincy fell 180 feet after slipping from a nineteenth-story balcony. According to her owner, Peter Thompson, who witnessed the mishap, Quincy luckily landed in a bush and suffered only a broken leg.

Ten days later, on May 1, a two-year-old cat named Gros Minou topped that mark with a record plunge of 200 feet from the twentieth-floor penthouse of his master, Dr. Eugene Trudeau of Outremont, Quebec, Canada. Fortunately, the cat slammed into a flower bed that cushioned his fall. Gros Minou sustained a fractured pelvis and was back walking within a few weeks—but not on the balcony.

Later that same year, on November 24, a female cat named Frankie nearly tied the record when she fell 195 feet off the nineteenth-floor terrace of her owner, Jane Kneeland of New York. Like the other two diving felines, Frankie was fortunate enough to have her fall broken by some foliage. She fractured her pelvis, but made a full recovery.

## Curiosity Nearly Killed the Cats

In several remarkable, documented cases, a curious cat wound up trapped for over a month without food and water—yet still managed to survive!

A stowaway cat lived after being accidentally locked in a shipping container holding a new Mercedes-Benz for an unbelievable forty-eight days.

In 1990, Maria Skartvedt bought the new luxury car of her dreams in London, England, for shipment to her home in Sydney, Australia. As the Mercedes was loaded into a huge container at a dockside warehouse, a cat wandered in and was sealed up with the car.

Nearly seven weeks later, the ship arrived in Port Adelaide, Australia. When the container holding the car was unloaded, workers were stunned to discover a black cat mewing weakly from behind the Mercedes. The feeble feline—nothing but skin and bones—was rushed to a pet clinic, where she made a complete recovery.

"She had no food at all and no water except some drops of condensation on the container's walls," said veterinarian Dr. John Holmden.

When the news hit the papers in Sydney, dozens of animal lovers offered to adopt the cat. But Maria, saying it was fate that brought the feline to Australia, claimed ownership . . . and named the cat Mercedes.

\*\*\*

Shadow, a blue point Himalayan, survived without food or water for thirty-seven days while she was trapped in a vending machine.

In 1990, Shadow disappeared shortly after her owner, Daresa Hooper of Grafton, Virginia, sold six empty snack machines to J.R. Hilton, owner of a vending business in nearby Chesapeake. Somehow, Shadow managed to sneak into one of the machines when Hilton removed the back to inspect the internal parts.

The five-foot-tall candy vending machine was transported to Chesapeake, where it was stored outside for more than a month under a tarp, awaiting resale.

Meanwhile, Daresa couldn't understand why her beloved cat was missing. She had searched the area and talked with neighbors, but no one had seen Shadow. Then, more than a month later, Daresa was struck by a thought. The last time she had spotted Shadow, the cat was sniffing around the vending machines that were being sold to Hilton. Daresa wondered, *Could Shadow have ended up trapped in one of them?* It seemed too ridiculous. But she had run out of ideas, so she called Hilton and asked him to inspect the machines.

He did. And sure enough, there was Shadow. "I opened the door to one of the machines and saw these two very blue eyes staring at me," recalled Hilton. "Then it let out three big yowls."

The cat had lost about three pounds during her ordeal. According to the veterinarian who treated the cat, "Shadow was thin and dehydrated, but amazingly bright and alert."

After being reunited with her feline friend, Daresa said, "The first day home, she had this worried look on her face like she couldn't understand why we hadn't come and gotten her weeks earlier. Happily, she's up to her old loving tricks."

### Fraidy Cat

A tiny, homeless kitten was accidentally sucked up in the vacuum hose of a city leaf-collection truck. Yet, incredibly, the kitty survived—without so much as a scratch!

In 1990, the little orange-and-white feline was foraging for food along a curb in Southington, Connecticut, when she became frozen with fear at the sight of the leaf-collection truck. By the time the operator saw the frightened cat, it was too late. The kitten was sucked up by the 175-mile-per-hour force of the truck's vacuum hose.

"Usually anything that goes in there is pretty much history," said Robert Taylor of the city street department.

When workers realized the machine had sucked up a kitten, they were horrified and thought they had killed someone's beloved pet. They dug about four feet into the truck's collection bin, but saw nothing. They then dumped the leaves out and carefully poked around with a rake, expecting to see a ghastly sight.

But to their surprise and joy, they found the kitten in a pile of leaves—unharmed! However, she was visibly shaken. "It looked like one of those Halloween cats with its hair standing straight up," Taylor said. "She was so scared. We just couldn't believe she was alive."

When city employees failed to find the kitten's owner, they declared the feline homeless. But rather than see her taken to the animal shelter, Charles and Lucia Klemovich, who lived near where the kitty was sucked up, agreed to take the cute feline into their home.

It didn't take them long to come up with a name for their new companion—Hoover.

*A cat can smell things ten times better*
*than a human can.*

## The Greatest Fall of All

On March 8, 1981, in Portland, Oregon, a despicable, coldhearted man threw a pregnant one-year-old black-and-white shorthair named Patricia off the St. John's Bridge.

The cat fell from a height of 205 feet into the frigid 49-degree Willamette River where she managed to tread water for several minutes before being rescued by two men who were fishing under the bridge.

It was the greatest documented height from which a cat has survived a fall.

Patricia was rushed to a pet clinic where examinations revealed she suffered from shock, multiple contusions, tears in her abdomen, a ruptured uterus, and severely bruised organs. The fall caused her to abort her three kittens, but she did survive.

Patricia was adopted by Fritz and Mardi Jacob, local directors of Pet Pride of Oregon, an animal advocacy group. Because of her ordeal, Patricia became a celebrity, making personal appearances at cat shows around the country.

## The Unsinkable Navy Cat

Oscar the tabby was either the luckiest sea-going cat ever . . . or the world's greatest jinx to sailors. He was the only cat ever known to have survived the sinking of three warships.

Born in Germany during World War II, Oscar was one year old when he became a feline crew member of the mighty battleship *Bismarck*. But in 1941, the pride of the German navy was sunk 660 miles off the coast of France. Oscar managed to leap into a life raft with some of the *Bismarck*'s crewmen, who were later picked up by the British destroyer HMS *Cossack*.

While his German comrades were made prisoners of war, Oscar was adopted by the British sailors aboard the *Cossack*. But later that same year, the destroyer was torpedoed. Once again, the cat was rescued from a watery grave, this time by the British aircraft carrier, HMS *Ark Royal*. The sailors aboard the carrier made him their mascot, but he didn't keep the title for long—only three days.

That's because, incredibly—for the third time during the war—Oscar wound up in the water when the *Ark Royal* was torpedoed by a German submarine in the Mediterranean. About three hours later, the bedraggled cat was spotted clinging to a floating plank by a British destroyer and taken ashore to Gibraltar.

Two weeks later, Oscar was taken off sea duty. He was shipped out to a sailors' rest home in northwest Ireland, where he lived out his life in tranquil surroundings.

*While writing in Key West, Florida, Ernest Hemingway kept more than a dozen pet cats—most of which had up to three extra toes.*

# *Lifesaving* Cats

## *...Who Rescued Others*

### Cat-Astrophe Averted

Charlie—an old, overweight, lazy, but lovable blue Burmese—turned into a hero when he saved his human family from a fiery death.

The ten-year-old feline normally stayed outside the home of Ken and Kimberly Coleman of Pensacola, Florida. But on the night of November 6, 1991, Charlie was allowed inside the house because the temperature had dipped into the low 40s. Charlie happily snuggled by the flames in the fireplace as the family watched television.

Shortly before midnight, after the Colemans had retired for the night, Charlie noticed smoke coming out of the fireplace. The alert cat then raced into the bedroom and pawed frantically at Kimberly's face until she woke up. Smelling the smoke, Kimberly awakened her husband, grabbed their two-year-old twins, called the fire department, and safely fled the smoke-filled house with her family—and with Charlie.

The fire, which started in the chimney, caused several thousands of dollars in damage and could have been a killer, had it not been for Charlie, said assistant fire chief Jim Rushing.

"Charlie knew we were in danger and saved our lives," declared Kimberly. "He'll never sleep outside again."

### Holy Catman!

Sparky, an unassuming four-year-old calico, turned into a raging lioness and rescued a helpless poodle from the deadly jaws of a pit bull.

Sparky was perched up on a ledge outside her home, napping in the sun one day in 1989 when owner Teresa Harper of Dora, Alabama, let her poodle, Lacy Jane, outdoors.

Seconds later, Teresa heard a tremendous commotion of growling and yelping. She rushed to the door and was shocked to see a savage, brown-and-white pit bull mauling poor Lacy Jane. "He had pinned her to the ground and was tearing at her throat," recalled Teresa.

Sparky, who was on top of the porch ten feet above the fray, gave an angry hiss and flew into action.

"She made a flying leap, just as pretty as you please," said Teresa. "Sparky landed right on that dog's head. She just clawed and scratched and clawed and scratched. He was bucking like a bronco but Sparky held on like a rodeo rider. Finally, he managed to throw her off and then ran off."

Teresa quickly scooped up the wounded Lacy Jane, who was bleeding badly from a gash in her neck, and raced her to the veterinarian.

"The poodle had a puncture wound on the right side," said Vicky Moorehead of the Sumiton Animal Clinic. "If that cat hadn't sent the pit bull running, Lacy Jane would have been killed. It's just amazing that such a small cat could be fierce enough to beat up a vicious pit bull."

*Cats saved millions of lives in the fourteenth century. When the knights returned from the Crusades, their ships brought back the Asiatic black rat, which carried and spread the bubonic plague—the Black Death. Twenty-five million people died of the plague before tens of thousands of cats were bred to kill off the rats.*

## One Man's Cat-tharsis

By his own admission, Bob Elion was living a dreary, lonely, depressing life. But all that changed when a little stray calico captured his heart.

"That cat literally saved my life," said Elion as he stroked his feline friend, who was cuddled peacefully on the patio deck chair at his condominium in West Boca Raton, Florida, during Thanksgiving weekend in 1991.

Elion, forty-five, had sold burial plots in Maryland before a chronic depressive illness cost him his job, his marriage, and his family in 1988. He hadn't worked since and stayed home alone most of the time, especially after his mother—his last living relative—died in 1989.

Then one night in June 1991, a special friend entered his life. While Elion was visiting Key West, a little calico followed him down the street. Elion kept shooing her away, but she kept coming back. His heart, which hadn't felt any emotion for two years, began to melt. Elion picked up the cute cat and brought her back to his lonely, empty apartment. He named her KeWe Fleming after the city and street where she found him.

Soon she became the center of his life. He bought special sleeping rugs for her in each room and made toys for her to play with. In return, KeWe gave him unconditional love.

A remarkable change came over Elion. "I became more outgoing," he said. "I began smiling and laughing. I hadn't had anyone to care for in a very long time. Now I was shopping for her and inventing things for her."

Life seemed worth living again. Elion's mental health improved. But then, the cuddly calico created a crisis that nearly plunged Elion into another deep depression.

An unfeeling neighbor complained that the condominium covenants didn't allow pets in the eighty-eight-unit complex of the Isles of Sandalfoot, where Elion lives.

The board of directors of the condo association agreed that Elion was in violation of the rules. KeWe would have to go. "I can't get rid of KeWe," Elion told the board. "She's like my family. She is my family. It's her and I."

Without KeWe, Elion knew he would sink into a deep, debilitating depression. In desperation, he turned to his therapist, Lois Latman, at the South County Mental Health Center. She wrote a letter to the condo association which stated, "It appears that his pet cat is helping him recover from the depression as much or more than any medication he is prescribed. We advise that he continue to keep his newfound friend as a live-in companion."

Based on the advice of an attorney for Benchmark Property Management Inc. of Coral Springs, Florida, which manages the complex, the board finally ruled on the case. It agreed to let KeWe stay, based on "humanitarian reasons."

So KeWe naps in her deck chair soaking up the sun, and Bob Elion sits nearby, smiling fondly at her. "Life is definitely worth living—with KeWe at my side," he said. "She's my lifesaver."

## Beagle Scout

Four kittens, who were only a week old when their mother was killed, survived—because they were nursed by a beagle!

The kittens were born in March 1992, outside the country home of Kirk and Rae Holliday of De Soto, Wisconsin. But days later, to the Hollidays' horror, the mother cat was run over by a car.

"We really didn't know what to do," recalled Kirk Holliday. So they brought the helpless kittens into the house and put them in a basket. The kittens mewed and huddled with each other while the worried family tried to figure out how they were going to feed them.

There was one family member who didn't have any problem figuring it out. Kai, a beagle mix, jumped right into the basket. "She took right over," said Holliday. "She just lay there with them that very first night and they started nursing on her."

The family was amazed, but realized that the beagle couldn't produce enough milk for her new feline family. So the Hollidays picked up formula from the vet and some doll-sized baby bottles to help feed the kittens and give Kai some help.

Said area veterinarian Tom Thompson, "It's rare that a dog would nurse kittens. It's kind of a neat thing, don't you think?"

## The Tabby that Turned Tiger

A lionhearted house cat attacked and drove off a vicious intruder who was beating a frail old woman. Thanks to the courage of the devoted feline, her life was saved.

On that fateful day in 1932 in Memphis, Tennessee, eighty-eight-year-old Nell Mitchell was ill and lying on a daybed in the kitchen of her modest home. Her favorite companion, a cat she named Shade McCorkle, was curled up at her feet on an afghan.

Suddenly, the sickly old woman heard the porch door open and footsteps coming toward her. She let out a gasp as the kitchen door swung open and a scruffy-looking, thin man in his early twenties stared coldly at her and said, "Lady, you got something to eat?"

Clutching the afghan up to her throat, the fearful Nell replied, "I'm too sick to help you."

The intruder grunted and his eyes darted around the room until they locked on Nell's hands. Menacingly, he stood over her and yelled, "Your ring! Give me your ring!" Frightened beyond belief, Nell tearfully pulled her cherished wedding ring off her finger. The man snatched the ring from her trembling hand and then, in a fit of unprovoked rage, struck her hard across the face.

As the assailant raised his hand to hit her again, Shade sprang into action. Baring his sharp claws and teeth, the tabby leaped onto the back of the man's shoulders. In a flash, the fourteen-pound feline fury lunged at the intruder's throat and, with a fearsome hiss, clamped down hard with his fangs.

The assailant hollered out in pain and whirled around the room, punching the ferocious cat. But Shade hung on, clawing and yowling like a banshee. "Call him off! Call him off!" the intruder cried.

Bleeding from the face and neck, he stumbled backward, knocking a table and a lamp to the floor. Finally, he managed to grab Shade by the throat and tried to strangle the cat. But Shade squirmed out of the man's suffocating grip and slashed at his face.

The assailant hurled the cat to the floor and staggered around the room, wiping the blood off his face with his shirt. But then, with renewed vigor, Shade leaped back on him and continued to claw and bite.

Screaming in agony, the man slammed Shade against a table and then made a mad dash out the door before the cat had a chance to launch another attack.

The police eventually caught the intruder and credited Shade with saving Nell's life. Meanwhile, both the elderly woman and her cat recovered from their bruises.

A group of pet lovers was so impressed with Shade's bravery in protecting his mistress that they presented the tabby with a gold medal for animal heroism.

*Cats have thirty teeth—twelve less than a dog*
*and two less than a human.*

# *Pampered* **Cats**

## *...Who Enjoyed the High Life*

### Happy Purrday, You Party Animal

It was flashier than many wedding receptions. Elaborate centerpieces. Scrumptious food. Door prizes. Live entertainment. Strawberries the size of golf balls flown in from California and hand-dipped in pink chocolate. And a cherry-filled cake with a bigger-than-life portrait of the guest of honor on the top.

So who was this important guest of honor? None other than a cat!

The $10,000 bash, held at the swank Palm Aire Hotel and Spa in Pompano Beach, Florida, in May 1991, celebrated the tenth birthday of an auburn Persian called Cherry Pop—winner of Best of Best, Cat of the Year, and many other prestigious national and international feline prizes.

Her beautiful red tail curled around her, Cherry Pop languidly lounged atop a table in a

cat-sized Rolls-Royce Corniche. She wore a mink-collared gold lamé cape made from the same fabric that was once used to create a coat for Marilyn Monroe.

As Cherry Pop purred, crooner Vic Sarno sang to her "Memories," the theme song from the Broadway musical *Cats*.

"If I could have afforded Barbra Streisand to come here to sing 'Memories,' I would have," said Huey Vanek, sixty-seven, the owner of Cherry Pop and a Florida-based dry-cleaning business profitable enough to let him throw such an extravagant party for a cat.

Added his wife, Vi, "Some people think we're nuts, but we don't care."

The couple's other two Persians—Leo Not The Lion and Fast Freda—get birthday parties too. But they've never had one as elaborate as this.

Cherry Pop seemed oblivious to the attention of the fifty guests who came to honor her. And why not? This is a cat who laps only Evian water, who sips wheat germ and skim milk from a spoon, and whose velvety paws have never touched asphalt. At dinner, she wears custom-made sequined bibs. She eats raw beef, slightly warmed to get rid of the chill, from a crystal bowl twice a day. "Only the best meat—round steak," Vi said.

Vi showed off her rhinestone-studded jacket with the cat's face painted on the back. She wore cherry-tinted glasses in the shape of Cherry Pop's face and sported a watch with the cat's portrait on it.

The Vaneks, who have no children, have willed their ten-room house to a cat lover. Upon their death, the beneficiary—whom they say will receive "enough money to never be able to spend it all"—will move into their house and care for Cherry Pop and her pals in the style to which they have become accustomed.

The Vaneks's house is adorned with cat posters, cat statues, cat plaques, cat cups, and cat houses, said Sarno, who has sung at birthday parties for the couple's other cats. "There are cat pictures everywhere," he said. "Vi and Huey are very nice, generous, unpretentious people. But when it comes to cats, they are just way out there."

In 1987 and 1988, the Vaneks spent $150,000 participating in cat competitions around the country. The couple, Cherry Pop, the two other Persians, and the cats' personal groomer flew first-class to cat shows. The Persians traveled in Louis Vuitton cat bags, stayed in five-star hotels, and ate in five-star restaurants. Cherry Pop once dined on carpaccio served on a silver tray.

Vanek turned down $50,000 from a cat lover who wanted to buy Cherry Pop. Recalled Vanek, "I told him, 'If you had a suitcase here with a million dollars in it, I wouldn't take it.'"


## Cat Heirs

It was the cat's meow for two Burmese cats. They inherited a fashionable $750,000 apartment!

Dark-brown felines Damon and Pythias were inseparable when their owner, wealthy widow Terry Krumholz, was alive. She made sure they would be together even after her death. Before she died in 1991, Mrs. Krumholz set up a foundation to care for the six-year-old cats, who shared her tenth-floor co-op in a luxury Fifth Avenue building in New York City.

"I think it's a wonderful thing she's done," said Dr. Lewis Berman, a veterinarian at Park East Animal Hospital.

In her will, Mrs. Krumholz gave the co-op to a foundation that she set up for the sole purpose of caring for Damon and Pythias. "During the life of the cats . . . the said cooperative apartment shall be held by the foundation as a home for the cats," her will stated. The foundation now pays for their care and feeding, as well as the monthly maintenance charge for the apartment.

Mrs. Krumholz's will named two caretakers and directed the foundation to consult with Dr. Berman and Carole Wilbourn, a cat psychology expert, regarding the cats' welfare.

Said Dr. Berman shortly after Mrs. Krumholz's death, "The cats were badly shaken up by the loss of Mrs. Krumholz. But they will be well taken care of."

\*\*\*

In 1978, house cat Charlie Chan was the beneficiary of a will signed by his mistress, Grace Alma Patterson of Joplin, Missouri, who left an estate worth $250,000 to her feline friend. The holdings included a three-bedroom house, a collection of antiques, and a seven-acre pet cemetery.

Charlie was looked after by a teacher who was allowed to stay in the house rent-free until the cat's death eight years later. "I couldn't have asked for a better landlord," said the cat's personal guardian. "He was just wonderful company and was absolutely no trouble. He had simple pleasures and never seemed to want anything else but his toys, his armchair, and his basket."

After Charlie died, the estate was auctioned off and the proceeds went to local and national humane societies.

\*\*\*

When Dr. William Grier of San Diego died in 1963, he left his entire estate, valued at $415,000, to his two fifteen-year-old cats, Hellcat and Brownie. The pets died two years later and the estate was given to George Washington University.

### Now *That*'s a Cat House!

A millionairess constructed a $100,000 guest house—solely for her pet cats!

In 1988, Francine Katzenbogen was a middle-aged, out-of-work beauty consultant who, with her brother and mother, cared for twenty stray cats that they had rescued from the streets of Brooklyn. Then one day that year, Katzenbogen bought her first New York State lottery ticket—and won $7 million!

By 1992, she decided to use the money to make her dream come true—to live out west in a ritzy house with all her cats. So Katzenbogen bought a $2 million estate on Laurel Canyon Boulevard in Studio City near Los Angeles. But even though the city code limits homeowners to three cats, Katzenbogen requested—and received—a variance from the city's zoning ordinance so she could build her precious felines a fancy home of their own.

"People may think I'm a crazy lady," said Katzenbogen. "Well, I'm not. I know what I'm doing. It's for my cats. If I want to spend my money and take care of my cats—which are my family—I don't think it's anybody else's business."

After the death of her mother and brother, Katzenbogen said she had no family left except for her cats. To ease her grief, she decided to move them to her fourteen-room, 5,894-square-foot mansion, complete with gym, tennis court, maid's quarters—and cat house.

"They are really like little people," said Katzenbogen, who flew her cats to California on a specially chartered flight after their new home was ready.

She spent $100,000 renovating the garage into an airy, 1,200-square-foot house with six rooms for her cats. The walls were painted a chic dove gray to complement the speckled Italian tile floors. The rooms were equipped with play towers and lounging platforms. Multi-paned French windows and skylights were installed so the cats "won't be bored," Katzenbogen explained. However, she added, shades can be drawn to shut out the sky so "they won't be scared by lightning."

After visiting the cat house, John Parica, an official of the zoning board that granted the variance, said, "We should all be so lucky to live that well."

*Cats were held in high regard in tenth-century Wales. According to the laws back then, if a husband and wife separated or divorced, the husband automatically gained custody of the family cat.*

## Fat Cat

Nathan N. Jones was one fat cat in 1992. He received in the mail a preapproved gold card, a $10,000 line of credit, and a sweepstakes check offering him $220, good toward the purchase of a sewing machine, matching his-and-hers diamond watches, or a Pierre Cardin five-piece set of luggage.

But the eight-year-old alley cat really wanted nothing more than a year's supply of tuna. "I tried to talk him into taking me to the south of France with that credit card," said Jim Bridges, a contractor who lives with Nathan in Seattle, Washington.

With no questions asked, the cat received his gold card after Bridges mailed in a coupon for some gourmet cat food samples he had seen offered in a magazine. Since the food was for Nathan, Bridges simply used the feline's name in the return address.

"It should be fun to see what other things Nathan will get in the mail once his name gets on other mailing lists," said Bridges.

*The heaviest domestic cat on record was a neutered male tabby named Himmy in Queensland, Australia. At the time of his death in 1986, he weighed a whopping forty-six-and-a-half pounds.*

## Pussies Galore

Jack and Donna Wright of Kingston, Ontario, Canada, lavish each cat they own with tender loving care—all 632 of them!

As a result, the cat-crazy couple spend a whopping $111,000 each year pampering their furry friends.

"Every day we feed them 180 cans of cat food, fifty pounds of dry cat food, and nine quarts of milk—which adds up to $256 a day, including kitty litter," said Jack. "Then we have a vet in every day for an average of $50 a visit. That's a total of $306 a day, or $2,142 each week.

"But every penny we spend on them is worthwhile. These cats are our children—and we'll sacrifice everything we own in the world to make sure they're happy."

The Wrights own a house-painting business that makes it possible for them to provide for all their "children."

Their cat collection began in 1970 when their only pet at the time, Midnight, had a litter of kittens. Since then, the Wrights have added to the number by rescuing strays and accepting cats from owners who want to get rid of them. "We're just softies where cats are concerned," said Donna.

By 1992, the Wrights were showering their affection on a whopping 632 cats, who have the run of the couple's modest two-bedroom house. Inside, the home looks like it's carpeted with live cats. The felines are on the refrigerator, stove, TV, couches, and even on the Wrights themselves, whenever they sit down.

But there's little time for Donna to rest. She puts in a ten-hour day caring for her pets. She scoops out seven litter boxes four times a day and disinfects floors and furniture three times daily. "We never take a vacation and I never go to the mall or even out for lunch with a friend," said Donna. "But I don't mind."

The Wrights are so in love with their cats that they know each one's name and personality by sight. At Christmas, every cat gets at least one present. And the couple even bakes twelve twenty-pound turkeys to feed the cats each Christmas, New Year's Day, Easter, and Thanksgiving.

Meanwhile, their feline family continues to grow—because Jack and Donna keep taking in abandoned cats.

*The most prolific cat on record was a tabby named Dusty of Bonham, Texas, who gave birth to a whopping 420 kittens from 1935 to 1952.*

# *Astounding* Cats

## *...Who Performed Amazing Feats*

### The Cat that Flew—On a Duck!

In one of the most astounding feats in feline history, a cat actually flew on the back of a wild mallard duck!

The cat, Kitty Boy, was not your average feline. In 1985, when he was only one week old, the orange-and-white tabby was found abandoned in the weeds by Maureen Neidhardt on the family cattle ranch near Richardton, North Dakota. Maureen nursed the infant feline with a doll's baby bottle.

As Kitty Boy grew older, he thrived on the ranch, hanging around with two Blue Heeler cattle dogs, Dingo and Penny. The dogs are a breed that snap at the heels of cattle to get them moving. Amazingly, Kitty Boy joined the canines in helping to round up the calves on the ranch. "The dogs patrolled the flanks while Kitty Boy brought up the rear," said Maureen. "He'd fluff up his tail as big as possible and then dash toward the calves, spooking them into running."

One evening in October 1986, her husband Marlin, their two dogs, and Kitty Boy set out across the pasture. Marlin wanted to check on a cow that he had rescued earlier in the day after it had fallen off a dam into a catchment area adjoining a lake. As the foursome neared the dam, they encountered a flock of mallard ducks resting by the edge of the water.

"Before I knew it, Kitty Boy had sprung for the mallards," recalled Marlin. "He spread all four of his legs as he dove after them. When he hit dead-center of the flock, the whole she-bang took flight. There was an awful explosion of quacking and flapping wings."

One of the birds was furiously beating its wings but getting nowhere fast. Finally, like an overloaded cargo plane, it slowly got airborne, and veered out over the lake about four feet above the water.

"I didn't realize what I was seeing at first," said Marlin. "I saw the duck listing and then I heard a meow."

That's when he saw a sight that he could never have imagined possible: There, clutching tenaciously to the back of the flying duck, was Kitty Boy!

"That cat was square on the duck's back, scared silly. He had wrapped his forelegs around the duck's neck in a death grip. I couldn't believe it."

The flustered, frantic bird kept flapping its wings in a desperate attempt to gain more altitude while the panic-stricken Kitty Boy wanted down. The duck turned around and made a low pass near the dam where Marlin, Dingo, and Penny were watching in awe.

Suddenly, Dingo leaped up and knocked the mallard out of the air. The duck crashed into some tall grass as Kitty Boy jumped off and scrambled under a bush to regain his composure. The mallard took off again, this time without its heavy load, and flew away in the night sky.

When the world's first feline duck-rider emerged from the bush, Marlin wondered whether anyone would believe what he had just witnessed. Recalled Marlin, "All I could think about was, 'How do I tell Maureen that Kitty Boy flew on the back of a duck?'"

## Climbing to Great Heights

A free-spirited cat with a lust for adventure became a legend in her time—by repeatedly climbing the Swiss Alps!

In 1928, a stray calico, who was later named Hilda, began tagging along with climbers who were trekking from the Swiss town of Kandersteg to the nearby mountain of Blumlisalphorn. Eventually, she made her new home at a mountaineering club's shelter at the 9,000-foot level, where she was fed by the guard.

But Hilda was not a feline who liked to sit still. One day, she followed a group of climbers who were making an ascent on the 12,038-foot peak. To their surprise, she accompanied the group all the way to the summit. (Naturally, there were points along the way where the climbers had to carry her.)

From then on, Hilda was known as Switzerland's mountain-climbing cat. She would sit outside the shelter, waiting for the next team of climbers to arrive. When they began their assault on one of the peaks, Hilda would be climbing right by their side.

**51**

Occasionally, Hilda chose to remain at the summit and refused to return with the group. She would play among the rocks and then surprise the next group of mountain climbers who arrived a few days later.

During one of her summit solos, a fierce snowstorm struck the peak and, sadly, Hilda was never seen again.

### That Dam Cat

One of the largest dams in the world was built with the help of a cat!

A cuddly little feline performed a task that no man could do to solve a major engineering problem in the construction of the mighty Grand Coulee Dam.

The dam, located on the Columbia River about 90 miles west of Spokane, Washington, is the largest concrete structure in the world. An impressive 550 feet high, the dam creates a reservoir that extends 151 miles, reaching the Canadian border.

In 1942, near the end of its nine-year construction, engineers ran into a little quandary. They were unable to thread a particular cable through 500 feet of a crooked and partially blocked drainage pipe that was less than a foot in diameter. But then one of the engineers saw a small, stray white cat that the work crew had been feeding every day—and he came up with a brainstorm. "I've got the solution!" the engineer shouted.

He picked up the friendly female cat. Then he attached one end of the cable to some heavy string and tied the string to the tail of the cat. Next, he placed the cat in the pipe. Thanks to her natural curiosity and a gentle blast of compressed air from behind, the cat ambled through the long pipe, dragging the cable behind her. When she reached the other end of the pipe, she successfully had threaded the cable.

The construction crew cheered and work continued on what is now one of the world's largest hydroelectric power installations. Unfortunately, the name and fate of the feline have been lost to history. Nevertheless, the nameless cat has remained a hero to the hard hats who built the Grand Coulee Dam.

## Purr-ty as a Picture

A pet cat named Bud D. Holly has pawed his way to artistic fame. The tabby paints abstracts—and hundreds have been sold, some for as much as $150!

In 1990, a stray, black-and-gray kitten showed up at the doorstep of Sharon Flood, owner of Village Art Gallery in Mendocino, California. Flood's heart melted and she adopted the feline. Since it was near Christmastime and she loved 1950s music, Flood named the cat after rock 'n' roll legend Buddy Holly.

At first, there was no inkling that the precocious kitten, who loved to roam from shop to shop and greet owners and customers, had any artistic talent. However, after one of his all-day forays, Bud returned home and left muddy paw prints on Flood's glass tables. That gave her an idea.

On a whim, she bought some nontoxic watercolors, put a few blobs onto paper, and let Bud walk around in the paint. "I did it as a joke," said Flood. "The paw prints looked great so I had him do some more."

After framing Bud's better works, Flood held a one-cat art show. To her amazement, the show was a cat-egorical success. Twenty paintings were sold that night from $15 to $125. "It all started as a thing to make people chuckle," said Flood. "But I found people actually like Bud's paintings."

Bud enjoys working with yellow, blue, and red watercolors. In addition to his paw prints, Buddy creates canvas splatters by shaking his paws. "With a little imagination, you can see things in his abstracts, such as teddy bears, ponies, and crocodiles," said Flood.

Said Mendocino sculptor Jim Niebel, "This cat is not to be ignored. He's a cat with incredible talent."

Added Flood, "When people come into the gallery and see Bud's work, they crack up. Then they try to get cute and say something like, 'My, aren't his paintings purr-ty.'"

## The Triathcat

Ziggy the cat holds the distinction of being the feline world's greatest triathlete, traveling almost 5,000 miles by canoe, backpack, and bicycle.

In October 1990, photojournalist Jim Adams hopped into his canoe and began the first leg of a year-long triathlon vacation. A few days later, Adams pitched camp on the banks of the Ohio River near Manchester, Ohio, when Ziggy—a two-month-old part Manx, part shorthair from a nearby farm—ambled over to him. The two struck up an instant friendship and, with the farmer's permission, Adams adopted Ziggy.

The gray kitten then embarked on a great adventure. He learned to walk along the gunnels of the canoe and sat in the bow like a veteran paddler. Even though cats supposedly hate water, Ziggy liked it—although he found that out the hard way. One day, while leaning over the side pawing at the boat's wake, he fell overboard. Once he realized he could swim, the cat became more adventurous around the water. Whenever they camped for the night, Ziggy would wade a couple of inches into the river and try to catch fish.

After his 2,000-mile trip down the Ohio and Mississippi rivers, Ziggy was ready for the second phase of the triathlon vacation—a 2,100-mile hike on the Appalachian Trail. He and Adams set out from Springer Mountain, Georgia, and trekked along the famous footpath through fourteen states.

Ziggy and Adams climbed up 5,000-foot-high peaks, slogged through wetlands, hiked in meadows, and walked along river banks all the way to Maine. With Adams carrying a forty-pound backpack, Ziggy happily tailed his companion, occasionally making side trips to pursue field mice, butterflies, and other small creatures. When it rained or when Ziggy got tired, the cat would jump onto the top of Adams's backpack for a free ride.

At their campsites, Ziggy often curled up close to the fire or kept warm by snuggling in the bottom of Adams's sleeping bag. When the weather turned wintry, Ziggy, unlike many cats, enjoyed romping in the snow.

When they were lucky enough to find one of the campers' shelters that dotted the trail, Ziggy would spend the evening catching mice. His record for one night was eleven.

For the final leg of their triathlon trek, the pair set out on a 900-mile bicycle trip from Bar Harbor, Maine, to Webster, Pennsylvania, where Adams's trip began. Ziggy loved to stand on one of the bike's saddlebags with the wind blowing in his face and his ears rearing back.

When they finally reached Webster a year after they had teamed up, Ziggy had completed a great American adventure. As the first feline known to have trekked the Appalachian Trail, the cat now looks forward to other camping excursions. Said Adams, "Ziggy knows the word 'camping' and when he hears it, he runs to the van, ready to go."

*While dogs may comprehend a human vocabulary of two hundred words, cats typically understand only about fifty.*

# *Curious* Cats

## *...Who Landed in Trouble*

**Cat Calls**

A curious cat got collared by the cops after she summoned them—by repeatedly dialing 911!

Police rushed to Barbara Marple's apartment to find out why 911 was being dialed without anyone speaking on the other end. Only then did they discover that the series of "cat calls" were coming from Barbara's feline friend, Kitten.

The first emergency call came on January 12, 1992, but the caller hung up without a word. Police traced the call to Barbara's apartment in Boynton Beach, Florida, and knocked on the door, but no one answered.

An hour later, another mysterious call was recorded, followed in rapid succession by several more. The police went back to the apartment and woke Barbara from a nap. The twenty-three-year-old

supermarket employee denied making the calls. So police investigated further. In a bedroom, they found her calico cat, Kitten, with one paw on the cordless phone. According to the police report, Kitten randomly punched 911 with her paw the first time and then an hour later she hit the redial button.

The police log reads: "Cat dialed 911 using auto redial. Case closed."

## Paws for Concern

A housecat single-pawedly cost an airline thousands of dollars in extra fuel, delayed passengers for three and a half hours, and caused others to miss their connections.

In 1990, Continental Airlines Flight 119 boarded fifty-three passengers for the two-hour trip from Fort Lauderdale, Florida, to Houston. But just after takeoff, the pilot of the Boeing 727 noticed a light on the control panel indicating that the heater to the cargo was not working. There was no danger to the plane or the passengers, but the captain still faced a life-or-death choice.

He knew that in the hold was a house cat in a carrying case belonging to one of the passengers. The air in the hold was growing deadly cold as the jet climbed. If the plane continued its ascent, the temperature in the hold would reach 50 degrees below zero and kill the cat.

So the captain turned the plane around and announced to the passengers that they were returning to Fort Lauderdale.

"The pilot said there was a mechanical problem and he certainly didn't tell us that the problem was a cat," recalled passenger Bob Schachner. "Only after we returned to the airport did we learn why we had come back.

"They opened up the cargo door and pulled out the carrying case to see if the cat was still alive. It was a tuxedo cat—black-and-white with a white stripe—and it was fine. The owner was so relieved."

Despite the cost to the airline and inconvenience to the passengers, the pilot was praised for his decision.

"It was just good customer care," said Ken Gordon, Continental's general manager at Ft. Lauderdale. "After all, I've got a cat, too."

*A cat's normal body temperature is 102.5 degrees Fahrenheit.
He doesn't begin to feel uncomfortable until the outdoor
temperature reaches 124 degrees.*

## A Shocking Tale

For four tense days, Finnegan the kitten sat atop a dangerous 60,000-volt power pole, afraid to come down, while firemen, animal control officials, and utility workers wondered what to do.

The kitty, owned by Shane and Miriam Cox of Sebastopol, California, climbed up the 60-foot pole one day in 1992—and then didn't know how to get down. Her frantic owners tried to coax her to the ground, but the scaredy-cat just sat there, meowing and looking forlorn.

The Coxes called the fire department and animal control officials, but they were afraid of being electrocuted and didn't attempt a rescue.

"We were at our wits' end," recalled Miriam Cox. At her urging, Pacific Gas and Electric Company sent a crew to see what it could do. The utility workers were concerned that in rescuing poor Finnegan they might accidentally interrupt power to the citizens of Sebastopol, a small town fifty miles north of San Francisco.

The crew tried four times to rescue the kitten, without success. But then the crew brought in a huge crane and maneuvered it safely around the lines and the pole.

A burly lineman volunteered to go up in the crane and—with a gathering crowd below cheering him on—managed to pluck Finnegan from his lofty hot seat to safety.

## Attack Cat

An outraged feline sought revenge on a family that supported a controversial cat licensing law.

In 1992, Bonni Matheson of Davenport, Washington, led support for a local ordinance calling for the licensing of feline pets. The city council began considering the pros and cons of such a measure.

Mrs. Matheson, who admitted she wasn't particularly fond of cats, found herself in the doghouse with at least one feline who wanted to sink his claws into the housewife.

A month before the council voted on the proposed ordinance, Mrs. Matheson was working in her yard in Davenport, minding her own business, when suddenly, "out of nowhere, came a white cat." She said the feline looked as if he were on a mission, singling her out for attack. The cat bit and clawed her hands, requiring treatment at the hospital.

Police Chief Jim Gants, using a skunk trap, captured the cat, which was taken to the local pound for a ten-day rabies observation. But two days later, the feline escaped—and, incredibly, made its way right back to the Matheson house!

Somehow the vengeful cat sneaked inside the house and then "it went right after us," recalled Mrs. Matheson. She said the cat tore up wallpaper in her kitchen and then took on the family's three dogs in the living room.

"My house was a total wreck," she said. "The kids and I got out of that house so fast it was unbelievable."

The cat was captured once again. This time, authorities made sure it wouldn't assault the Mathesons. He was put to sleep.

But the cat attack apparently wasn't in vain. The city council voted against the feline licensing law.

As for Mrs. Matheson, the specter of the attack cat continued to haunt her. "I had a nightmare that the cat rang my doorbell," she told reporters, "and when I opened it, the cat said, 'I'm baaack!'"

*More than one hundred pet cats with heart problems have had pacemakers implanted in them. The devices were obtained from people who had died or were new ones with slight defects that didn't affect their performance.*

## Litter Laws

Cats have given legislators plenty to fret about over the years. Several municipalities have enacted cat curfews, leash laws, and licensing ordinances. But some measures seem absolutely ridiculous. For example:

In Zion, Illinois, it's illegal to give a lighted cigar to a cat.

Natchez, Mississippi, passed a law making it illegal for a cat to drink beer.

Melbourne, Australia, imposed that country's first curfew on cats. Residents have to lock up their feline friends from 8 P.M. to 6 A.M.—or pay a $78 fine.

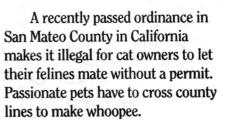

A recently passed ordinance in San Mateo County in California makes it illegal for cat owners to let their felines mate without a permit. Passionate pets have to cross county lines to make whoopee.

In 1949, bird lovers successfully propelled a leash law for cats through the Illinois state legislature. However, Governor Adlai Stevenson vetoed the bill, concluding, "The problem of cat versus bird is as old as time. If we attempt to resolve it by legislation, who knows but that we may be called upon to take sides as well in the age-old problems of dog versus cat, bird versus bird, or even bird versus worm."

## No Pussyfooting Around

A judge curbed a mischief-making pet cat—by placing him under house arrest!

The roving rascal—an orange-and-white feline named Mortimer—was barred from the outdoors in 1989 after his owner's neighbors in Calgary, Alberta, Canada, filed a lawsuit for damages they claimed the tiny terror caused to their property.

The trouble started in 1983 soon after Al and Ann Marshall moved into the neighborhood where Mortimer lived with his owner, retired firefighter Garry Huskinson.

"Mortimer made our lives miserable," Mrs. Marshall told reporters. "He dug up the vegetables in our garden, used our potted plants for a litter box, and even climbed through windows into our house and through vents into our greenhouse."

One year, according to the lawsuit, the frisky feline ruined an Easter dinner for the Marshalls. "Mortimer managed to get into the house and we found him munching on ham with potato salad and pie all over the floor," said Mrs. Marshall. "My husband suffers from asthma and I'm allergic to cats, so we had to go to the hospital after our house was invaded. We found balls of his orange-and-white hair under our beds."

In 1988, the Marshalls became so fed up with Mortimer that they had him picked up by the local Society for the Prevention of Cruelty to Animals. Only then did Huskinson receive from his neighbors a long list of transgressions that the cat had committed. "Mrs. Marshall accused Mortimer of doing everything except knocking her house down," said Huskinson. "I was shocked. I knew Mortimer was a roamer, but I had no idea he was causing this kind of problem."

The following spring, Huskinson received another shock when the Marshalls filed a $30,000 lawsuit against him and two other neighbors who owned cats, claiming the animals were damaging their property.

Before the case was scheduled for trial, a judge felt the allegations were so serious that he put Mortimer under house arrest. Huskinson was ordered to keep the cat indoors at all times, except for an occasional furlough when he could walk the feline, on a leash only.

Eventually, the lawsuit was settled. However, Mortimer's roaming days were over. Said Huskinson, "He's on the end of a forty-foot leash and his pussyfooting days are definitely behind him."

### Feline-ious Assault

Smokey the cat went on trial for assault, but was acquitted after hundreds of people showed up as character witnesses for the defendant.

For years, Smokey, an old Russian blue, was a fixture at J.R. Weldin Co., Pittsburgh's oldest office supply store. He loved to sit on top of the cash register at the front of the store and get treats and pats from customers. "People sometimes came in just to see Smokey," said store owner Peg Brown. "They'd have their picture taken with him and he would ham it up."

But in 1987, lovable Smokey was charged with assault.

Customer Nickki Sikorski, a nineteen-year-old legal secretary, claimed that the old cat badly scratched her when she tried to buy tape for her boss. So she filed a $3,000 negligence suit against the store in small claims court. According to her boss, Richard Johnson, the attorney who handled her case, the scratches on Nickki's left hand made her look "like a heroin addict." Johnson was asking for $1,500 in damages for "psychological discomfort, shock, and dismay" and $1,500 in medical costs.

"We were convinced that Smokey didn't do it," said Mrs. Brown. "He was too sweet. Besides, no one saw it happen."

When the local media ran stories about the case, it became something of a *paws celebre* in Pittsburgh. Three area attorneys volunteered to represent Smokey for free.

"Even though we had insurance, customers insisted that we set up a Smokey Defense Fund," recalled Mrs. Brown. "So we put a jar by the cash register next to Smokey and customers put in dimes and quarters. People sent us letters with checks from as far away as Australia! We ended up collecting over $1,400." (The money was eventually donated to various animal charities.)

On the day of the hearing before three arbiters, so many of Smokey's friends showed up planning to testify on his behalf that the proceedings were moved to a bigger courtroom. "Hundreds and hundreds of people were there to back Smokey," said Mrs. Brown. "It was wonderful."

Both sides fought the case tooth and nail. The plaintiff's lawyer introduced photos of Nickki's scratched hands and invoked a local ordinance against harboring an animal in a place of business.

Brown and other workers testified that Nickki never said a word about the alleged attack at the time it was supposed to have taken place. Testimony about Smokey's gentle nature and friendliness filled the courtroom.

The arbiters took less than two hours to deliberate. In a unanimous decision, they announced in favor of the feline. Smokey was absolved of all guilt and Nickki was ordered to pay all court costs.

## Marriage Cat-Aclysm

A housewife loved cats so much that she eventually was caring for more than one hundred of them at home. Finally, her fed-up husband gave her an ultimatum: either the cats go or he goes.

She didn't hesitate for a second. She gave him her answer—and away he went.

In 1974, Christine Ann Thomas—whose initials spell CAT—started caring for a few cats after a back injury left her unable to walk. However, the former psychiatric nurse of Wakefield, England, got better as her passion for felines grew.

By 1991, her two-bedroom house was littered with thirty cats, with another ninety-nine in two heated sheds in her backyard. Cleaning and feeding the residents of her kitty commune began at 6 A.M. and didn't end until midnight. That didn't leave much time for Christine to spend with Billy, her husband of sixteen years.

Billy, a gardener, finally had enough of living with a house full of cats. "I really got the impression she thought more of the cats than she did of me," Billy told reporters.

"Christine spent all our money on the cats—$300 a week on cat food, plus hundreds on veterinary bills." He said the tabby tab became a financial burden that he could no longer handle.

So when Billy told her, "It's either me or the cats," the feline fanatic didn't even pause to think about it—and sent him packing. "By leaving, he simply created more room for me to take in more cats," said Christine.

### All's Wall That Ends Wall

A stray cat found what she thought was the perfect place to have her litter—inside the wall of a house!

But she caused the homeowner plenty of grief and worry.

In 1992, the mama, a black-and-white stray, slipped through an unscreened attic vent in the roof of the home of Fran Carlton of Lake Clarke Shores, Florida. The cat then selected a cool place inside a wall near an air conditioning duct and gave birth to four kittens.

They remained quiet as their mother nursed them. But after a few weeks, the kittens began meowing loud enough for Fran to hear them behind the wood-paneled wall of her family room. She had hoped the cat would take the litter outside her house. But as the days went by, it was clear the feline had no intention of moving the kittens.

"Whenever the kittens stopped meowing for a while, I panicked," Fran recalled. "I just hoped and prayed they were sleeping. Then I worried that they were trapped for good and would die there."

Finally, she asked a friend and general contractor, Jon Spradley, to help retrieve the kittens. Spradley took off the baseboard, reached in, and captured one of the kittens. He left the board off, hoping the others would crawl out, but they didn't.

So a week later, Spradley bent the wooden paneling back within inches of cracking it and reached in as far he could. One by one, he pulled three more healthy kittens from atop a stud beam. "When we finally got them out, I was so excited. It was like I was having them myself," said Fran.

The kittens, dazed after spending their month of life behind a wall, each weighed only a few ounces and were about four weeks old. Fran found homes for all of them. A few days after the kittens were retrieved, the mama cat disappeared.

The kitty rescue was not Spradley's first. In 1989, while building a Palm Beach mansion, he and his workers had to chip through a $3,500 marble-tiled Jacuzzi they had just installed to rescue a litter of kittens.

"Fran's was certainly a cheaper job," he said.

# *Courageous* Cats

## *. . .Who Left Their Paw Prints on History*

### The Cat Who Earned the Medal of Honor

A black-and-white tomcat named Simon received a distinguished war medal from Great Britain.

In 1948, when Simon was still a kitten, he was given as a gift to Lt. Commander I.R. Griffiths, commanding officer of the British frigate HMS *Amethyst*, which was then stationed in Hong Kong. The cat quickly won the hearts of the crew and was given the run of the ship, where he proved to be a first-class rat-catcher.

Life was great for Simon. He had plenty of food, companionship, and exercise. But then, in the spring of 1949, trouble brewed.

The army of Red China swept victoriously across the mainland and gained control of much of the Yangtse River. The *Amethyst* was quickly dispatched to the city of Nanking to protect British lives and property there. While on its way, the frigate was ambushed, coming under heavy gunfire from batteries of the Chinese Communist Army firing from both sides of the river.

One of the shells landed in the quarters of Commander Griffiths, killing him instantly. Simon, who was in the same room, sustained serious injuries from shrapnel and a badly singed coat. The cat managed to stagger out of the room and slipped into hiding to lick his wounds.

Meanwhile, the crippled *Amethyst* ran aground on a mud bank as fifty-four crewman lay dead or seriously wounded from the attack. Rather than go in for the kill and sink the ship, the Red Army put a blockade around the frigate and began negotiations with the British government for its release.

Three days after the barrage, a limping Simon came out of hiding and returned to duty. He once again was killing off rats that, because of the shelling, had emerged from the recesses of the frigate and threatened the health of the surviving crew members. Simon performed his mission tirelessly as negotiations between the British and Chinese Communists dragged on for three months.

In his daily reports to the British naval base in Hong Kong, the ship's radio operator often included a mention of Simon's efforts. News of the tough cat eventually made headlines throughout the British empire.

Finally, with fuel oil and food desperately low, the *Amethyst* broke the blockade under the dark of night and made a 168-mile life-or-death dash to the safety of the South China Sea. When the ship arrived back in Hong Kong, the crew and Simon received a tumultuous welcome. In fact, Simon was showered with gifts from admirers all over the world who had read about his courage.

But the injuries during the attack had taken its toll on the feline, and three weeks after the repaired *Amethyst* returned to England, Simon died. A war medal for bravery was presented to him posthumously on April 13, 1950, for "meritorious and distinguished service."

## You Gotta Have Faith

A sweet female tabby named Faith displayed such incredible courage that she became a morale booster for millions of Britishers during the Battle of London.

At the outbreak of World War II, Faith was living in the rectory of St. Augustine's Church, next to St. Paul's Cathedral, and slept in her own special basket on the top floor. During one of the nightly bombing raids on London, the cat gave birth to a black-and-white kitten that the rector named Panda. The proud mama was very protective and would put her paws around her newborn at the sound of the first bomb exploding in the distance.

The rector noticed that about a week after giving birth, Faith seemed uncharacteristically restless. With her tail down, she went from room to room as if searching for something. Finally, she returned to the top floor where Panda was sleeping in his basket, picked him up by the scruff of his neck, and carried him down to the basement. There, she curled up with Panda in a cubbyhole where old music sheets were stored.

Just three days later, on September 9, 1940, the rectory received a direct hit from a German bomb. The building collapsed in a fiery explosion. But as walls crumbled and flames raged, Faith huddled as far back in the recess as she could, shielding little Panda from the blazing inferno.

The following morning, the rector searched through the smoldering rubble, praying for a miracle that the felines somehow had survived. Suddenly, he heard a faint mewing. Frantically, he cleared the debris and there, still in the recess and covered with dust and soot, were Faith and Panda—unhurt!

The mother's courage throughout her terrifying ordeal made front-page news in the London newspapers and became a morale booster to the British who were under nightly siege.

Although Faith could not be awarded a military medal for bravery because she was a civilian cat, a special silver medal was struck and presented to her along with a certificate acknowledging her "steadfast courage in the Battle of London."

Today the certificate hangs in the church alongside a picture of a brave tabby named Faith.

**Insurance Claws**

Cats were so valuable to sailing vessels years ago that without the felines, shipping companies risked losing thousands of dollars.

Maritime insurance companies recognized the value of cats in protecting the ships' stores of grain and food from rats. Insurance companies viewed the absence of a cat onboard as negligence on the part of the captain. As a result, if the ship had no cat, the insurance company wouldn't pay any claims for grain or food damaged by rats.

**The Day the Egyptian Army Was Defeated—by Cats!**

Many scholars believe that cats actually led to the defeat of the Egyptian Army in 525 B.C.

During their war with Persia, the Egyptians had thwarted the attack of the Persian king Cambyses II, son of Cyrus II the Great, in a battle at Pelusium. The invading Persians were beginning to lose heart.

Then Cambyses came up with a brilliant idea. He ordered his soldiers to search all over the countryside for cats and seize as many felines as they could find. Cambyses's troops thought he was nuts, but they followed his orders.

The soldiers returned with hundreds of cats. Three days later, Cambyses launched an attack against the Egyptians. But rather than wave their swords as they approached the enemy, the Persian troops were each ordered to hold up a cat.

The Egyptians were stunned. They revered the cat as a god. In the temples, the high priests would watch cats day and night for omens based on the way felines slept, walked, stretched, and moved their tails and whiskers. Cats were held in such high esteem that if the family cat died, the family shaved off all their eyebrows and went into deep mourning. At adolescence, children had a cat's silhouette tattooed on their arms to call down the blessing of Bast, the cat god, on their lives.

During the Persian War, Cambyses knew the Egyptian soldiers considered the cat a sacred animal. Because of their belief, they refused to shoot their arrows at Cambyses's troops for fear of harming the felines. The Egyptians were helpless and their leader in the battle, Psamtik, surrendered without a single blow exchanged. Cambyses then continued on and, with the help of the kidnapped cats, sacked Memphis and returned to Persia triumphant.

**Puss 'n' (Combat) Boots**

A tomcat was pressed into service to help Russian soldiers during the fierce battle of Stalingrad in 1942.

During the shelling of the city by the German army, a stray cat found refuge inside the bunkered headquarters of a Russian company commander. The cat proved to be a morale booster for the men, who named him Mourka and shared their meager food rations with him. Often, the cat would saunter outside, but once the big guns began blazing away, he would scurry back to HQ for cover.

Communications between the forward gun positions and headquarters was spotty at best. So the commander drafted Mourka for hazardous duty. Knowing that the cat would hightail it to HQ during battle, the commander would give the feline to one of the gun crews near the front. When the fighting became too dangerous for human runners, the gunnery crew chief would write a message, attach it to Mourka's collar, and let him loose.

The brave cat would then scamper back to the company headquarters with the message intact and be rewarded with a bite of food and a friendly pat. Mourka performed his mission courageously for several months before, sadly, he was declared missing in action.

### Blood, Sweat, and Cats

At a particularly bleak period for Britain during World War II, Winston Churchill's pet cat did his part for the war effort.

The prime minister's feline friend Nelson—named after the famous British admiral, Horatio Nelson—was often by his master's side. The ginger tomcat sat in on cabinet meetings and was personally carried by Churchill to the bomb shelter whenever London was attacked.

At the time, the British were on very limited rations, attempting to conserve everything from fuel to food supplies. A British government official went to call on Churchill to discuss some important policy matters and found the prime minister in bed, recovering from the flu. Nelson was curled up at the foot of the bed.

After listening to the official complain about the problems he was encountering with his job, Churchill blew his nose, pointed to Nelson, and thundered. "That cat is doing more for the war effort than you are! He is acting as a hot-water bottle and saving us fuel and power!"

*Because cats can see so well in the dark, the U.S. Army experimented with them during the Vietnam War. Cats were put on leashes to lead foot soldiers through the night jungles. But the felines were a flop. They hated their leashes, chased after bugs, and refused to trek in the rain.*

**Frequent Flyer**

Adolph the cat logged more than 90,000 miles of flying during World War II for the U.S. Army Air Corps.

In 1945, Capt. Ed Stelzig of the 5th Squadron, Second Combat Cargo Group, was sent to Darwin, Australia, to pick up a group of officers on leave. While the pilot was resting on the tarmac in the shadows of the wings, a black-and-white stray kitten suddenly jumped into his lap. The kitty was so affectionate that the pilot decided to keep him.

Everyone who saw the feline laughed at his funny-looking face. His head was almost all white except for a little black patch beneath his nose that looked like the shape of German dictator Adolph Hitler's mustache. So Stelzig named his furry friend Adolph. The captain put a litter box in the rear of the plane, made his cat an honorary copilot, and let him fly on all his missions.

During the flights, Adolph slept on the radio equipment because it was always warm and comfy. At the end of each mission, the cat would jump out of the plane, explore the airstrip, and wouldn't return until he heard the sound of the engines of Stelzig's plane starting up.

Only once did Adolph miss a flight with Stelzig during the entire Pacific campaign. The feline boarded the wrong plane and ended up 500 miles away from Stelzig's destination. But cat and captain were eventually reunited and Adolph never made that mistake again.

When Stelzig received his orders to return home after the war, he presented Adolph to the children of a retired colonel. They had fallen in love with the flying feline—a seasoned veteran who had logged 92,142 documented air miles.

### Me-ow, My, What Kind of Music Is That?

One of the most bizarre musical instruments ever invented required the help of cats in order to play it.

During the sixteenth century, a device called a cat organ became a popular streetside diversion throughout Europe.

Trained cats were placed inside a beautifully decorated box with their tails poking through different holes. The cat organ player would make "music" by giving gentle tugs on the tails to elicit various meows.

Sometimes larger boxes were constructed, holding as many as sixteen cats at a time. With the aid of an assistant, the "musician" would pull different tails to play a symphony of meows.

*A cat can hear sounds up to two octaves higher than those heard by a human, and another half-octave higher than a dog. A feline can hear frequencies from 20 Hertz to 50,000 Hertz, putting his hearing in the ultrasonic range. Humans cannot hear beyond 20,000 Hertz.*

# Celebrity Cats

## ...Who Achieved Feline Fame

### The Fabulous Flying Felines

Spot, Piggy, Mars, and Sharkey are just average alley cats except for one thing—they have gained international fame for performing amazing feats of derring-do.

They have been headliners at Walt Disney World's Pleasure Island at Lake Buena Vista, Florida, where they leap from stool to stool, jump high in the air, stand on their front legs, and even soar through flaming hoops.

The fabulous flying felines—all four are mongrels—were no more born or bred for a career in show business than their owner, middle-aged Frenchman Dominique Lefort.

On a visit to Florida in the early 1980s, Lefort watched circus people practice their craft in Sarasota. He was enthralled by clowns and animal acts, especially the lions and tigers.

He began working as an independent clown performing at birthday parties and other functions when one day he spied a kitten in a pet shop window. It was love at first sight. He bought the feline and named her Marlene.

Even though he had been told that cats are basically so independent and lazy they can't be trained to perform tricks, Lefort tried to incorporate Marlene into his clown act. At first, she was a disaster. But Lefort persevered.

Soon he and Marlene had perfected their act to the delight of audiences in Key West, Florida. For one trick, she sat in a miniature circus wagon, reached out with her claws and popped a balloon. Then she ran to a stool, stood up, and raised her front paws in a "ta-da!" gesture. Man and cat were even featured on "Late Night with David Letterman" and other TV shows in the U.S., Spain, and Japan. Meanwhile, Marlene had kittens, which Lefort named Mars, Spot, Piggy, and Sharkey.

In 1988, however, tragedy struck. Marlene was killed by a pack of dogs after she slipped out of the house. To help ease his grief, the heartbroken clown decided to train Marlene's offspring in the hope that they would share the spotlight that was once hers alone.

Now they're stars in their own right. But like all other house cats, they constantly show their independence—even during the middle of a show. During a typical performance, Mars makes an awe-inspiring leap, stops, licks his paw, looks around, meows, and resumes his licking. Spot stalls before a trick to scratch his neck. And Piggy begins grooming herself on stage, pauses for a second as Lefort tells her to stop, and then she proceeds to clean herself.

*If you are a cat lover, then you are an ailurophiliac.*

## Gus, the Theater Cat

Gus isn't a performer or actor, but he has full command of the Church Street Theater in Washington, D.C. In fact, the gray tabby cat saunters out on stage whenever he likes—most often during scenes that don't call for a cat.

The alley cat made his impromptu theater debut in 1986 in the second act of the production of *Life and Limb*. It was a brief—and totally unexpected—cameo appearance during a performance for the press. Gus's stage presence garnered chuckles from the audience—and then a mention in the next day's reviews.

Because he doesn't have any agent telling him what roles he can or cannot take, Gus loves to saunter down the catwalk and into the middle of a play whenever the mood strikes him. Once in 1988, during a production of *Faulkner's Bicycle*, he leaped onto the stage and then into the audience.

Often, only the audience is aware of Gus's presence because the actors are so involved in their performances. After one of his stage appearances that the actors failed to notice, actress Brigid Cleary lamented, "If I had seen Gus, I could have ad-libbed that I looked like something the cat had dragged in."

No one knows why the alley cat decided to make the theater his life. He started coming around in 1984. Whenever the stage door was left open, the feline would run inside and hide underneath the stage, refusing to leave until the stage manager—who didn't like cats— chased him out with a broomstick.

Two years later, in 1986, a new stage manager, Dan Kiernan, welcomed the cat and treated him like one of the crew. The friendly feline established the furnace room as his quarters and had full run of the theater.

One of the actors decided to name the pet after the hero of the poem "Gus The Theatre Cat." The verse appears in T.S. Eliot's *Old Possum's Book of Practical Cats,* from which the musical *Cats* was adapted.

"We all are willing to pitch in and take care of Gus," said producing manager Cheryl Svannack. "There are many mornings when we come in and there's no coffee, but there's always cat food for Gus."

The happy tabby has been an unwitting set designer and teacher's aide for acting students. When the feline left paw prints on a freshly painted set, designer William Kelley was delighted with the cat's artwork.

Gus sometimes shows up at training sessions for acting students, said artistic director Peter Frisch. "A number of times he has suddenly appeared on stage, and I tell the students to incorporate him into the scene. The sudden appearance of a cat provides the ideal opportunity for improvisation."

Added actor Nick Olcott, "Gus has a better instinct for finding the best light and best center of stage than most actors."

***

Hassan Kamy, Egypt's leading tenor, says he has been upstaged by cats many times during a performance.

"The most memorable incident happened in the last act of *La Boheme*," he recalled. "I was holding the dying Mimi in my arms. The orchestra was silenced for the finale. Then a cat walked on stage. At first, the audience giggled. But the cat took its time getting across and I kept holding Mimi. Finally, the audience was hysterical—and so were Mimi and I."

## The Mews-Worthy Mayors

Since 1987, every mayor of Guffey, Colorado, has just pussy-footed around. And no wonder. All the mayors have been cats!

For years, Guffey, located near the New Mexico border in Park County, sported a post office, a two-room schoolhouse, a service station, and a general store. It was home for seventeen people.

Betty Royce, the local deputy sheriff, became fed up with local and county officials who seemed to ignore Guffey's needs for better roads and a town hall. "We might as well have a cat for mayor, as much good as it would do us," Royce complained.

So that's just what the good folks of Guffey did. In 1987, they appointed a white cat named Paisley as their mayor! County officials considered the appointment an insult. But the press considered it mews-worthy and stories about the four-footed mayor spread throughout the country.

Thanks to the media coverage of Mayor Paisley, the county paid more attention to Guffey and put in some badly needed roads. But before much else was done, Paisley died of old age after serving one year in office.

So the citizens of Guffey appointed another feline to the post, this time a Persian and Siamese mix named Smudge LaPlume. (Her last name was in honor of her beautiful tail, which she waved behind her as she walked.) Smudge did a pretty good job. Soon, Guffey had other roads and bridges repaired by the county.

But fate intervened, and poor Mayor Smudge LaPlume was assassinated by a coyote before she had served out her term.

Guffey then drafted another feline for mayor—a calico imported from Canon City, forty miles away. But the cat needed a name.

When the children of Wink, Texas, read about the new mayor of Guffey, they decided to run a cat-naming contest for the rookie officeholder. An elementary school made it a class project. Soon other residents of Wink joined in with their own suggestions.

A special nominating committee in Guffey received seventy-eight letters from Wink, offering their choices on what to call the new mayor. After spirited discussion, the folks in Guffey announced the winning name for their mayor: Wiffey LaGone.

The moniker was conjured up by Wink sixth-grader Patrick Gray, who wrote, "Drop the Gu in Guffey and put in the Wi from Wink and then, in honor of the past mayors who had gone to their rewards, add the last name of LaGone." In appreciation for coming up with the winning name, Guffeyites awarded Patrick a Guffey General Store sweatshirt.

Mayor Wiffey LaGone has been in office for several years now and has done Guffey proud. The county has built a community center to handle the needs of the population, which has increased to twenty-six.

"The residents love their mayor," said Joe Whiteman, owner of the general store.

"We've gotten action out of the county on some badly needed projects that we couldn't get them to budge on before. The progress came from having a cat for mayor.

"She handles her job like most other mayors. She kisses babies and greets visitors. She sleeps, eats, goes out—and fools around. Yesiree, she does an excellent job."

*The Nippon Crown Record Company of Japan began selling a compact disc in 1992 to help cats relax. The CD contains six slow and calm instrumental tunes featuring woodwinds as well as a bassoon and cello. The music is mixed with stress-relieving sounds for cats, such as purring and buzzing flies.*

### Miss Divine Feline

Princess Kitty is her name and chasing fame is her game.

This former alley cat sports a couple of elegant party dresses and a matching feather hat. Sometimes she wears a brown business suit or school dress, tailored to fit by her personal designer.

Princess Kitty also has her own fan club, her own bank account, and her very own telephone number. She's been written up in on the front page of the *Wall Street Journal* and pictured in full color in *Newsweek*.

Since 1988, this fantastic feline has been performing tricks for tens of thousands of schoolchildren and pediatric patients—and she loves every minute of it.

"Princess Kitty likes to be admired and to hear applause," said her owner, Karen Payne, a former newspaper reporter. And the cat has received plenty of accolades.

To the astonishment of professional animal trainers who believe it's hard to teach cats anything, Princess Kitty performs about seventy different tricks in her repertoire. Among them: playing part of the tune of "Three Blind Mice" on a toy piano—and slam-dunking a mini-basketball!

In 1986, Princess Kitty was an orphaned, stray kitten that wandered onto Payne's patio. Because the kitten wouldn't stop biting, Payne found a book about training house cats. She taught the cat to stop biting and then worked on other basics of obedience, such as stay, come, sit, and lie down. To Payne's surprise, the cat learned quickly—and seemed to enjoy it.

"She's taken over my life," said Payne. "She taught me how to act as a cat trainer so she could show off all the things she can do."

It didn't take long for Princess Kitty to get her act together. Ever since word of her talent spread, she's been performing in front of delighted children at schools and in hospitals. Remarkably, she's unfazed by an auditorium full of rowdy children who shout and clap. She just laps up the attention. Kids have been so enthralled with her talent that they not only have joined her fan club but they also send her letters, poems, and artwork.

She's appeared in television miniseries—her best role was playing Ernest Hemingway's favorite cat—and has shown off her talents on talk shows throughout the country.

"Princess Kitty is the ambassador of her species," said Payne. "She represents cats and the fact that they can do and be more than people ever thought was possible."

Adds Moura Steinberg, president of Princess Kitty's fan club: "She's an inspiration to a lot of people. She's proof that a common little alley cat can become a princess."

*The oldest breed found in North America is the American Shorthair, the ancestors of which crossed the Atlantic with the early settlers. At least one cat is reported to have sailed with the Pilgrims on the Mayflower in 1620.*

### A Fair-Weather Friend

Fridays are special for feline lovers in Portland, Oregon. That's the day when Bob the Weather Cat appears on local TV station KATU.

While most stations show beautiful sunsets or breathtaking scenery as backdrops to their forecasts, KATU shows Bob. The sixteen-pound gray mixed breed dresses for the weather. For instance, he gets decked out in sunglasses and a sailor suit if sunshine is predicted, or wears earmuffs and a scarf if snow is on the way. He also gets dolled up for special occasions. Every Christmas, he dons a red outfit as Santa Claws. When members of the Bolshoi Ballet were in town, he was ready for a *paw de deux* in tutu and ballet slippers.

Bob was just a typical stray cat in 1983 when he was adopted by the family of KATU news cameraman Bob Foster. In 1985, while trying to come up with a picturesque weather shot, Foster filmed the cat sitting under a tree. Audience reaction was so good that Bob has appeared on almost every Friday weathercast since.

"People tune in to see what he's going to wear," said Foster. "We've had him in more than 300 different outfits. He's been dressed up as an angel, a jogger, a lion and, for Mother's Day, a mom. Once Bob was the feline version of Elvis with a wig, sideburns, and a white jumpsuit. We've also had him decked out in a basketball jersey in 1992 when the Portland Trail Blazers were in the NBA Finals."

Bob the Weather Cat has been so popular that his image adorns bumper stickers, buttons, and greeting cards. He's received thousands of letters—including several marriage proposals from feline fans.

"Bob's been a big hit with viewers and it looks like he'll have a long TV career," added Foster. "So far, he's outlasted three TV weathermen, five news anchors, and three general managers."

*The tabby—a cat with dark stripes running down the spine and whorls on the flanks—got its name from the ancient Persian empire. The fur resembled richly colored silk or taffeta that was originally made in Attabiah, Iraq. People who noticed the similarity between these kinds of cats and the fabric started calling the felines Attabiah. Eventually, the name was shortened to tabby.*

## Cat-ering to the Public

Cats are acting as official greeters in many public buildings. For example:

Herbie, a tiger-striped feline, welcomes visitors to the Herbert Hoover Presidential Library in West Branch, Iowa. The cat winds himself around the legs of guests on the porch of the thirty-first president's birthplace.

The feline was a stray who showed up at the doorstep of the attraction. Workers fell in love with him and gave him the name of Herbie in honor of the former president.

Herbie sleeps in his own white, shingled cottage—a mini-replica of Hoover's home, right down to the chimney, windows, and covered entrance. It even sports wall-to-wall carpeting! "Every day I see people kneeling down, trying to get a picture of Herbie in his home," said Thomas Walsh, executive director. "He's very popular with the visitors."

\*\*\*

In 1981, a friendly black stray checked into Bethesda Memorial Hospital in Boynton Beach, Florida, and has stuck around ever since.

The feline, named Lady, greets staff and visitors alike at the hospital's entrance. She comes and goes as she pleases, using the hospital's automatic doors. "She stays pretty much outside the front door or in the lobby," said her friend, Janet Dicks, a hospital official.

"Lady brings a smile to everyone. She offers comfort, too, for the families of patients. One time, a therapist put her in the lap of a stroke victim and the patient beamed and uttered her first sound since her stroke. We all love Lady."

\*\*\*

For thirteen years, a gray cat named Jaws was an official jail house cat who greeted women prisoners.

In 1975, when she was a tiny gray kitten, Jaws scampered through an open door of the Sacramento (California) County Jail and hid in the women's booking room. The kitty was booked under California Penal Code Section 647 (g)—trespassing.

From 1975 to 1988, Jaws—so named because she nipped at the fingers of people who played too rough with her—welcomed each new female inmate by rubbing herself against the prisoner's leg. Interestingly, in her thirteen years on duty, Jaws never once ventured to other floors, where male inmates were kept.

### The Aristo-cat-ic Actor

No feline has a longer list of television and movie credits than S.H. III–known as "the Cary Grant of cats."

Suave and debonair, the chinchilla Persian loves to pose quietly and regally to show off his white coat with the distinctive gray shaded ticking and the natural black mascara that lines his eyes.

But when the cameras roll, the veteran twelve-year-old feline actor does everything asked of his owner, Hollywood animal trainer Scott Hart (after whom the cat is named). S.H. III can retrieve, stand on his hind legs, stop on a mark, touch a prop, wave, box, hiss, walk on command, and perform almost any action that the role requires.

All this talent and beauty has made S.H. III much in demand. He's appeared in such TV shows as "The Rockford Files," "Dynasty," and "Punky Brewster." And he's been in such films as *The Jerk, Scrooged, National Lampoon's Christmas Vacation,* and *Strays.*

But the role that catapulted him to stardom is the cat in the Fancy Feast TV commercials. He's usually seen eating his cat food dinner out of a delicate Waterford crystal dish.

A kitten star, S.H. III began his acting career at the age of nine weeks, working under Hart. "In 1982, Friskies PetCare Products was looking for a cat with beauty, grace, an air of sophistication, and with the unmistakable touch of elegance," Hart recalled. "S.H. III fit that bill perfectly.

"Ever since, he's become a big star, mostly because of his inherent feline sex appeal. He's been likened to 'the Cary Grant of cats.' It's also his charm and ability to understand and respond to many verbal commands."

When he's not acting, S.H. III makes guest appearances at cat shows across the country. At each event, he presides over the presentation of the Fancy Feast Cup, given to the highest-scoring feline in the show.

All of this attention has not spoiled S.H. III, according to Hart. However, the cat, who shares Hart's southern California home, does eat his dinner in a crystal dish.

*Centuries ago, in what is now Thailand, when a member of the royal household died, a Siamese cat was entombed alive with the body. But the feline didn't die. Holes were dug large enough for the animal to escape. Attendants waited outside the tomb and recaptured the cat. The feline, symbolizing that the soul of the dead person had been freed, was then carried to a special temple where it was pampered for the rest of its life.*